BIBLE STUDIES

Living Like You Belong to God

Kay Arthur, David & BJ Lawson

PRECEPT MINISTRIES INTERNATIONAL

WATERBROOK
PRESS

Living Like You Belong to God
Published by WaterBrook Press
12265 Oracle Boulevard, Suite 200
Colorado Springs, Colorado 80921

ISBN 978-0-307-45866-7
ISBN 978-0-307-45867-4 (electronic)

Published in the United States by WaterBrook Multnomah, an imprint of the Crown Publishing Group, a division of Random House Inc., New York.

WATERBROOK and its deer colophon are registered trademarks of Random House Inc.

Printed in the United States of America
2012

10 9 8 7

CONTENTS

HOW TO USE THIS STUDY

This small-group study is for people who are interested in learning for themselves more about what the Bible says on various subjects, but who have only limited time to meet together. It's ideal, for example, for a lunch group at work, an early morning men's group, a young mothers' group meeting in a home, a Sunday-school class, or even family devotions. (It's also ideal for small groups that typically have longer meeting times—such as evening groups or Saturday morning groups—but want to devote only a portion of their time together to actual study, while reserving the rest for prayer, fellowship, or other activities.)

This book is designed so that all the group's participants will complete each lesson's study activities *at the same time*. Discussing your insights drawn from what God says about the subject reveals exciting, life-impacting truths.

Although it's a group study, you'll need a facilitator to lead the study and keep the discussion moving. (This person's function is *not* that of a lecturer or teacher. However, when this book is used in a Sunday-school class or similar setting, the teacher should feel free to lead more directly and to bring in other insights in addition to those provided in each week's lesson.)

If *you* are your group's facilitator, the leader, here are some helpful points for making your job easier:

- Go through the lesson and mark the text before you lead the group. This will give you increased familiarity with the material and will enable you to facilitate the group with greater ease. It may be easier for you to lead the group through the instructions for marking if you, as a leader, choose a specific color for each symbol you mark.

- As you lead the group, start at the beginning of the text and simply read it aloud in the order it appears in the lesson, including the "insight boxes," which appear throughout. Work through the lesson together, observing and discussing what you learn. As you read the Scripture verses, have the group say aloud the word they are marking in the text.

- The discussion questions are there simply to help you cover the material. As the class moves into the discussion, many times you will find that they will cover the questions on their own. Remember, the discussion questions are there to guide the group through the topic, not to squelch discussion.

- Remember how important it is for people to verbalize their answers and discoveries. This greatly strengthens their personal understanding of each week's lesson. Try to ensure that everyone has plenty of opportunity to contribute to each week's discussions.

- Keep the discussion moving. This may mean spending more time on some parts of the study than on others. If necessary, you should feel free to spread out a lesson over more than one session. However, remember that you don't want to slow the pace too much. It's much better to leave everyone "wanting more" than to have people dropping out because of declining interest.

- If the validity or accuracy of some of the answers seems questionable, you can gently and cheerfully remind the group to stay focused on the truth of the Scriptures. Your object is to learn what the Bible says, not to engage in human philosophy. Simply stick with the Scriptures and give God the opportunity to speak. His Word *is* truth (John 17:17)!

LIVING LIKE YOU BELONG TO GOD

In today's churches, the concept of *holiness* seems a bit archaic, or "old school." On the rare occasions the word *holy* comes into conversation, most people picture a preacher in a robe or a woman wearing a long skirt and her hair in a bun—individuals whose lives are devoid of fun, joy, and laughter.

Perhaps you associate the concept with an offensive holier-than-thou attitude sported by some self-appointed member of the piety police. Or does the word *holy* bring a sense of defeat and discouragement at the thought of the perfect life you know you will never attain?

Our goal in this study is to turn those misguided notions on their heads and help you see that in fact a life of true holiness is the key to true happiness. Rather than some arbitrary standard set by the church or an unreachable goal of sinless perfection, holiness is about pleasing God, about living in such a way that it's clear you belong to Him. Holiness is what makes the believer unique and easily distinguishable from the unbeliever.

Although it's been neglected in recent years, holiness is a biblical idea, one that is mentioned over six hundred times in the Bible. It is even the key theme for some of the books in the Bible, such as Leviticus. If holiness is such a basic biblical concept, then we should know what it is and what it is supposed to look like in our lives.

In the next six weeks we will learn what holiness is, what God thinks about it, and how the practice of holiness should guide the daily life of a believer.

Although some people prefer to believe that a loving God looks upon all His creatures as being the same, from the very beginning He has chosen to set certain things and people apart from others. This week we'll look at some of the clear distinctions God has set to mark specific people and things as holy.

OBSERVE

As we begin our study we need to go back to the Creation account in order to see who God is and what His desire was from the very beginning.

Leader: Read Genesis 1:1–5 aloud. Have the group say aloud and...

- *mark every reference to **God**, including pronouns, with a triangle:* △
- *draw a cloud shape like this* ☁ *around the word **separated**.*

As you read the text, it's helpful to have the group say the key words aloud as they mark them. This way everyone will be sure they are marking every occurrence of the word, including any synonymous words or phrases. Do this throughout the study.

GENESIS 1:1–5

¹ In the beginning God created the heavens and the earth.

² The earth was formless and void, and darkness was over the surface of the deep, and the Spirit of God was moving over the surface of the waters.

³ Then God said, "Let there be light"; and there was light.

⁴ God saw that the light was good; and God separated the light from the darkness.

⁵ God called the light day, and the darkness He called night. And there was evening and there was morning, one day.

DISCUSS

• Look at where you marked *God* in this passage and list out all that He did.

• So you don't miss it, what specifically did God separate?

• Isn't that exciting? The first recorded words of God are "Let there be light." His first act was to separate the physical light from the physical darkness. And spiritually speaking, He has been separating light and darkness ever since. Keep that in mind as we continue our study on holiness.

OBSERVE

The people of Israel, God's chosen nation (Genesis 12), had been slaves in Egypt. God chose a man named Moses to lead them out and to serve as a mediator between them and Himself. The passage we're going to look at begins after God's chosen people had sinned greatly against Him. He forgave the sin but threatened to withdraw His presence from them. So Moses was pleading with God.

Leader: Read Exodus 33:15–16 aloud.

• *Have the group draw a cloud around the word* **distinguished:** ⌒⌒

EXODUS 33:15–16

15 Then he said to Him, "If Your presence does not go with us, do not lead us up from here.

16 "For how then can it be known that I have found favor in Your sight, I and Your people? Is it not by Your going with us, so that we, I and Your people, may be distinguished from all the other people who are upon the face of the earth?"

DISCUSS

• What did Moses say distinguished Israel from all the other nations?

• So with that in mind, what did Moses want more than the knowledge the nation was forgiven?

• What about you? Would you be content to simply know your sins are forgiven, or do you want more than that? What distinguishes you from the world around you?

OBSERVE

As outlined in Leviticus 21, the priests were expected to preserve the holiness of the sanctuary and the uniqueness of the people of Israel. Therefore, they were subject to a higher standard than the average Israelite.

LEVITICUS 21:6

They shall be holy to their God and not profane the name of their God, for they present the offerings by fire to the LORD, the food of their God; so they shall be holy.

DEUTERONOMY 33:10

They shall teach Your ordinances to Jacob, and Your law to Israel. They shall put incense before You, and whole burnt offerings on Your altar.

Leader: Read Leviticus 21:6 and Deuteronomy 33:10 aloud. Have the group say and…
- *put a* **P** *over each occurrence of the word* **they,** *referring to the* **priests.**
- *draw a cloud around the word* **holy.**

INSIGHT

The word *profane* here means "to defile, make common, dishonor, to violate a covenant."

DISCUSS

- What did you learn from marking the references to priests? What were they responsible for?

OBSERVE

Israel had not obeyed God's laws, and the priests were partly to blame.

Leader: Read Ezekiel 22:26 aloud. Have the group…
- *put a* **P** *over each reference to* **priests,** *including pronouns.*

- *draw a cloud shape like this* ☁ *around the words* **holy** *and* **clean.**
- *draw a cloud with a slash through it over the words* **profane** *and* **unclean,** *like this:* ☁

DISCUSS

- What charges did God, speaking through Ezekiel, bring against the priests?

- We have seen that the priests were to teach Israel the difference between the clean and unclean. They were taught in Leviticus how they were to live in order to be an example to the nation. From all we have seen so far, were the priests following God's commands? Explain your answer.

- How seriously does God take making the distinction between holy and profane, and why?

EZEKIEL 22:26

Her priests have done violence to My law and have profaned My holy things; they have made no distinction between the holy and the profane, and they have not taught the difference between the unclean and the clean; and they hide their eyes from My sabbaths, and I am profaned among them.

LEVITICUS 10:1–5

¹ Now Nadab and Abihu, the sons of Aaron, took their respective firepans, and after putting fire in them, placed incense on it and offered strange fire before the LORD, which He had not commanded them.

² And fire came out from the presence of the LORD and consumed them, and they died before the LORD.

³ Then Moses said to Aaron, "It is what the LORD spoke, saying, 'By those who come near Me I will be treated as holy, and before all the people I will be honored.'" So Aaron, therefore, kept silent.

OBSERVE

As we've seen, it was the duty of the priests to guard the holiness of the nation. By strict obedience to God's law, they showed themselves to be separate and made a clear distinction between holy and unholy.

Leader: Read Leviticus 10:1–5 aloud. Have the group...
- *underline the references to **Nadab** and **Abihu.***
- *mark every reference to **the Lord,** including pronouns, with a triangle:* △

INSIGHT

Nadab and Abihu had been privileged to stand on the holy mount with Moses and their father (Exodus 24:9). Having heard the words of the Law, they knew what God required.

DISCUSS

- Were Nadab and Abihu doing what the Lord had commanded? Explain your answer.

• How does verse 1 describe the fire that they used?

• Was that a problem? Why?

• From what you have seen so far, how would you describe the attitude of Nadab and Abihu?

• Was God pleased with their worship? How did He respond?

INSIGHT

Fire from heaven is used twelve times in the Old Testament—six times as a sign of God's approval and six times in judgment.

In this context *holy* means to be set apart from the common and to be treated with great respect. The priests treated God as common and with great disrespect.

• God took Nadab and Abihu's disobedience seriously. Discuss how this relates to us today.

4 Moses called also to Mishael and Elzaphan, the sons of Aaron's uncle Uzziel, and said to them, "Come forward, carry your relatives away from the front of the sanctuary to the outside of the camp."

5 So they came forward and carried them still in their tunics to the outside of the camp, as Moses had said.

• What was God's command in verse 3?

• Can you walk in disobedience and be in His presence?

• Can you enter God's presence without regard to His holiness? Explain your answer.

ROMANS 15:4

For whatever was writ-ten in earlier times was written for our instruction, so that through perseverance and the encourage-ment of the Scriptures we might have hope.

OBSERVE

The Old Testament passages we've looked at so far make clear God's concern with separating holy from profane in ancient times. But we need to know whether such distinctions still apply today. Let's look at some New Testament passages to find out.

Leader: Read Romans 15:4.
  • *Have the group say aloud and draw a squiggly line under the word* ***written:***

DISCUSS

• What did you learn from marking *written,* and how does it relate to our study?

OBSERVE

What does all of this talk about priests have to do with us?

Leader: Read 1 Peter 2:5, 9. Have the group say aloud and…
- *circle each occurrence of the pronoun **you**, which refers here to **believers**.*
- *draw a cloud around the word **holy**.*
- *put a P over the word **priesthood**.*

INSIGHT

The word *priesthood* here carries the idea of a fraternity, a body of priests. It is referring to all believers.

DISCUSS

• What did you learn about believers from these verses?

• According to verse 5, as priests what are they called to do?

1 PETER 2:5, 9

5 You also, as living stones, are being built up as a spiritual house for a holy priesthood, to offer up spiritual sacrifices acceptable to God through Jesus Christ.…

9 But you are a chosen race, a royal priesthood, a holy nation, a people for God's own possession, so that you may proclaim the excellencies of Him who has called you out of darkness into His marvelous light.

ROMANS 12:1–2	OBSERVE

ROMANS 12:1–2

¹ Therefore I [Paul] urge you, brethren, by the mercies of God, to present your bodies a living and holy sacrifice, acceptable to God, which is your spiritual service of worship.

² And do not be conformed to this world, but be transformed by the renewing of your mind, so that you may prove what the will of God is, that which is good and acceptable and perfect.

OBSERVE

Although Jesus' death on the cross ended the need for blood sacrifices once and for all, Christians today are still expected to present sacrifices to God. Let's look at how this ties in to the call to be different from the world around us.

Leader: Read Romans 12:1–2 aloud. Have the group say and…

- *circle the pronouns **you** and **your**, which refer here to **believers**.*
- *draw a cloud around the word **holy**.*

DISCUSS

• As a priest, each believer has the incredible privilege of coming into the presence of God, but with that privilege also comes responsibility. What are the responsibilities of the believer-priest?

• If the believer-priest does this, what will the result be? Explain your answer.

OBSERVE

Let's look at two more passages that highlight the responsibilities of believer-priests.

Leader: *Read 1 Peter 1:14–16 and Ephesians 5:6–10. Have the group say aloud and...*
- *circle the pronouns* ***yours, your, yourselves, and you.***
- *draw a cloud around the word* ***holy*** *as well as the phrase* ***you shall be holy for I am holy.***
- *draw a box around the words* ***former*** *and* ***formerly:*** ⬜

DISCUSS

- What did you learn about believer-priests in these verses?

- How does what you see in these verses relate to what we saw earlier in this lesson regarding God's people making a distinction between the holy and unholy?

1 PETER 1:14–16

14 As obedient children, do not be conformed to the former lusts which were yours in your ignorance,

15 but like the Holy One who called you, be holy yourselves also in all your behavior;

16 because it is written, "You shall be holy, for I am holy."

EPHESIANS 5:6–10

6 Let no one deceive you with empty words, for because of these things the wrath of God comes upon the sons of disobedience.

7 Therefore do not be partakers with them;

8 for you were formerly darkness, but

now you are Light in the Lord; walk as children of Light

9 (for the fruit of the Light consists in all goodness and righteousness and truth),

10 trying to learn what is pleasing to the Lord.

• From all we have seen this week, what is the connection between separation and holiness? What does it look like to be separate?

• As we bring this lesson to a close, discuss how the truths you've seen have impacted you and how that will shape your personal choices.

• How does the way we handle these truths affect our representation of Jesus in the world?

WRAP IT UP

The first recorded words of God in Scripture are "Let there be light" (Genesis 1:3). His first recorded act, after creating the heavens and the earth, was to separate light from darkness. This actual physical separation became a metaphor for a spiritual truth. In John 1, Jesus is described as the Light of the world shining into the darkness. In Matthew 5, Jesus taught that, as citizens of the kingdom of heaven, believers are the light of the world (verse 14). "Let your light shine before men in such a way that they may see your good works, and glorify your Father who is in heaven" (verse 16). Jesus then went on to describe holy living in the rest of the Sermon on the Mount (Matthew 5–7).

Light is to be the characteristic of Christians. We are to be clearly separated from the darkness. No gray, no shade, no shadows. We, as people who name the name of Christ must be light—bright pure light, shining in the darkness so that everyone will see the truth and some will even seek our Father.

Are you living as a child of light? Is your holiness clearly visible to a dark world?

Sometimes, in too many places, the people called the church are living in the shadows. Spend some time in prayer, asking God to show you areas of darkness in your own life, areas where you are not walking in holiness. If God shows you an area of darkness, confess it as sin, knowing that He has promised to cleanse you from all unrighteousness.

Then walk in light; live out the holiness that shows you belong to God.

God chose Israel as His own people. He entered into covenant with them and called them to be a holy nation. They were to be His people, sanctified and separated from the other nations.

But what does it mean to be holy? What was to be their standard? What would set them apart? And finally, what difference do the answers to these questions make for us?

OBSERVE

Before Moses led the nation of Israel out of Egypt, he worked for years as a shepherd. The following passage describes what happened while Moses was pasturing his father-in-law's flock and approached Mount Horeb, also known as Mount Sinai.

Leader: *Read Exodus 3:2–6 aloud. Have the group say and…*

- *mark every reference to **God**, including pronouns and synonyms such as **Lord** and **angel of the Lord**, with a triangle:* △
- *draw a cloud shape like this* ☁ *around the word **holy.***

EXODUS 3:2–6

2 The angel of the LORD appeared to him in a blazing fire from the midst of a bush; and he looked, and behold, the bush was burning with fire, yet the bush was not consumed.

3 So Moses said, "I must turn aside now and see this marvelous sight, why the bush is not burned up."

4 When the LORD saw that he turned aside to look, God called to him from the midst of the bush and said, "Moses, Moses!" And he said, "Here I am."

5 Then He said, "Do not come near here; remove your sandals from your feet, for the place on which you are standing is holy ground."

6 He said also, "I am the God of your father, the God of Abraham, the God of Isaac, and the God of Jacob." Then Moses hid his face, for he was afraid to look at God.

DISCUSS

• Describe how the Lord appeared to Moses according to verse 2 and the circumstances surrounding this incident.

INSIGHT

The phrase *angel of the LORD* is usually considered to refer to a physical manifestation God or of Christ.

Fire was often a symbol of God's presence, such as when He later descended on Mount Sinai (Exodus 19:18).

• What did God say to Moses?

• Discuss why Moses responded to God the way he did.

• This is the first time the word *holy* is used in Scripture. What is described as holy?

• Why was it holy or what made it holy?

OBSERVE

On the same mountain where He met with Moses in a burning bush, the holy God is about to create a separate people by making a covenant with them.

Leader: *Read Exodus 19:1–6 aloud. Have the group say and mark the following:*

- *every reference to **God,** including synonyms and pronouns, with a triangle.*
- *every reference to **the sons of Israel,** including synonyms and pronouns, with a star of David:* ✡

Leader: *Read Exodus 19:1–6 aloud a second time. This time have the group...*

- *draw a cloud around the word **holy.***
- *underline the phrase **My own possession.***

DISCUSS

- According to verse 1, when did this event take place?

- Discuss what you learned from marking the references to God in this passage.

1 In the third month after the sons of Israel had gone out of the land of Egypt, on that very day they came into the wilderness of Sinai.

2 When they set out from Rephidim, they came to the wilderness of Sinai and camped in the wilderness; and there Israel camped in front of the mountain.

3 Moses went up to God, and the LORD called to him from the mountain, saying, "Thus you shall say to the house of Jacob and tell the sons of Israel:

4 'You yourselves have seen what I did to the Egyptians, and

how I bore you on eagles' wings, and brought you to Myself.

5 'Now then, if you will indeed obey My voice and keep My covenant, then you shall be My own possession among all the peoples, for all the earth is Mine;

6 and you shall be to Me a kingdom of priests and a holy nation.' These are the words that you shall speak to the sons of Israel."

INSIGHT

A covenant is a formal, binding agreement made between two parties, with both parties assuming some obligation. In this case it is between God and Israel.

• Under this covenant, what was God's obligation?

• What was Israel's obligation?

DEUTERONOMY 28:9

The LORD will establish you as a holy people to Himself, as He swore to you, if you keep the commandments of the LORD your

OBSERVE

Leader: *Read the following passages, ending with Psalm 147:19–20. Have the group say aloud and...*

> • *mark with a star of David every reference to **the people of Israel**, including synonyms such as **Jacob** and the pronoun **you**.*

• *underline the following phrases:* ___people to Himself, peoples to be Mine,___ *and* ___His own possession.___

• *draw a cloud around the word* **holy.**

Leader: *Read the passages aloud once more, without pausing to mark anything.*

DISCUSS

• Discuss what you learned from marking the references to Israel.

LEVITICUS 20:26

Thus you are to be holy to Me, for I the LORD am holy; and I have set you apart from the peoples to be Mine.

DEUTERONOMY 7:6

For you are a holy people to the LORD your God; the LORD your God has chosen you to be a people for His own possession out of all the peoples who are on the face of the earth.

PSALM 135:4

For the LORD has chosen Jacob for Himself, Israel for His own possession.

God and walk in His ways.

PSALM 147:19–20

19 He declares His words to Jacob, His statutes and His ordinances to Israel.

20 He has not dealt thus with any nation; and as for His ordinances, they have not known them. Praise the LORD!

• So you don't miss it, what is unique about Israel according to Psalm 147?

EXODUS 19:10–12, 21, 24

10 The LORD also said to Moses, "Go to the people and consecrate them today and tomorrow, and let them wash their garments;

11 and let them be ready for the third day, for on the third day the LORD will come down on Mount Sinai in the sight of all the people.

OBSERVE

The God of the universe was about to make a covenant with His people. Let's return to Exodus 19 and look at God's instructions to Moses for preparing the people of Israel to be consecrated—set apart to Him as a holy nation.

Leader: Read Exodus 19:10–12, 21, 24 aloud. Have the group ...

*   • *mark all references to **the people**, including the pronouns **them** and **you**, with a star of David.*

• *draw a box around the words **beware, warn,** and **do not let:*** ☐

DISCUSS

• According to verses 11–12, what was God going to do and what did He want Moses to do?

• Discuss God's warning to the people and the consequences if they didn't heed it.

• From what you have seen so far, how would you say God must be approached, and why is that true?

12 "You shall set bounds for the people all around, saying, 'Beware that you do not go up on the mountain or touch the border of it; whoever touches the mountain shall surely be put to death.' "...

21 Then the LORD spoke to Moses, "Go down, warn the people, so that they do not break through to the LORD to gaze, and many of them perish."...

24 Then the LORD said to him, "Go down and come up again, you and Aaron with you; but do not let the priests and the people break through to come up to the LORD, or He will break forth upon them."

EXODUS 15:11

Who is like You among the gods, O LORD? Who is like You, majestic in holiness, awesome in praises, working wonders?

1 SAMUEL 2:2

There is no one holy like the LORD, indeed, there is no one besides You, nor is there any rock like our God.

ISAIAH 6:3

And one called out to another and said, "Holy, Holy, Holy, is the LORD of hosts, the whole earth is full of His glory."

REVELATION 4:8

And the four living creatures, each one of them having six wings,

OBSERVE

Let's take a look at the character of the God who called Israel—and later us—to be His own.

Leader: Read the following verses aloud, starting with Exodus 15:11 and finishing with Revelation 15:4. Have the group mark...

- *every reference to **God** and **the Lord**, including pronouns, with a triangle.*
- *the words **holiness** and **holy** with a cloud.*

INSIGHT

The root of the Hebrew word for *holiness* means "to separate." The idea is that of separation between what is unclean and what is pure, between what is common and what is sanctified. God is separate from all that is evil and defiled. His holy character is the standard for moral perfection. Therefore holiness for us is simply conforming to the character of God.

DISCUSS

• Discuss what you learned about God and His holiness from these verses.

---

are full of eyes around and within; and day and night they do not cease to say, "Holy, holy, holy is the Lord God, the Almighty, who was and who is and who is to come."

REVELATION 15:4

Who will not fear, O Lord, and glorify Your name? For You alone are holy; for all the nations will come and worship before You, for Your righteous acts have been revealed.

OBSERVE

Now we've seen that holiness is a vital attribute of God. This same quality is to be a characteristic of His people. Holiness is the standard not only for the Israelites but for all who claim Him as their God.

LEVITICUS 11:45

For I am the LORD
who brought you up
from the land of Egypt
to be your God; thus
you shall be holy, for I
am holy.

LEVITICUS 19:2

Speak to all the
congregation of the
sons of Israel and
say to them, "You
shall be holy, for I
the LORD your God
am holy."

1 PETER 1:15–16

15 But like the Holy
One who called you,
be holy yourselves also
in all your behavior;

16 because it is writ-
ten, "You shall be holy,
for I am holy."

Leader: *Read the following verses aloud,
ending with 1 Corinthians 3:16–17. Have
the group say and…*

- *mark each occurrence of the word **holy**
  with a cloud.*
- *draw a triangle over every reference to
  God, including pronouns and synonyms
  such as **the Lord** and **the Holy One.***

DISCUSS

- What did you learn from marking *holy* in
  these verses?

• From what you have seen in these verses, what is to be our standard of behavior?

1 Corinthians 3:16–17

16 Do you not know that you are a temple of God and that the Spirit of God dwells in you?

17 If any man destroys the temple of God, God will destroy him, for the temple of God is holy, and that is what you are.

OBSERVE

A holy people in covenant with the holy God must never forget who they are and the separateness they are called to.

Leader: Read Numbers 15:37–41 aloud. Have the group…
   • *mark each reference to **tassel(s)** with a* **T.**
   • *underline the phrases **remember all the commandments** and **remember to do all My commandments.***
   • *draw a cloud around the word **holy.***

Numbers 15:37–41

37 The LORD also spoke to Moses, saying,

38 "Speak to the sons of Israel, and tell them that they shall make for themselves tassels on the corners of their garments throughout their generations, and that they shall put on the tassel of each corner a cord of blue.

39 "It shall be a tassel for you to look at and remember all the commandments of the LORD, so as to do them and not follow after your own heart and your own eyes, after which you played the harlot,

40 so that you may remember to do all My commandments and be holy to your God.

41 "I am the LORD your God who brought you out from the land of Egypt to be your God; I am the LORD your God."

DISCUSS

• What was the purpose of the tassels?

• Why was it important for the people of Israel to remember the commandments?

• Although we don't sew tassels on our garments today to help us remember the commandments and to do them, what tangible reminders do you use to prompt yourself to read the Scriptures and to do what they say?

WRAP IT UP

God is holy. God is separate from and other than all of creation. There is none like Him, there is none beside Him. He is righteous, He is pure, He is holiness dwelling in unapproachable light (1 Timothy 6:16). The song of heaven is "Holy, holy, holy is the Lord God Almighty who was, who is, and who is to come" (Revelation 4:8).

If this is our God, how should we as His people live and reflect His glory in a dark and dying world? How do we live as a holy people, as a kingdom of priests, as image bearers of the Almighty?

We represent God by walking in obedience to His commands. The two greatest commands are to love God and to love people. As we seek God through the study of His Word, we fall more and more in love with and in awe of the Lord. His command is then to love the people in the world as He loved us.

It is a great privilege to be a child of God. But with privilege comes responsibility. It is our responsibility to conduct ourselves in a manner that reflects God's holiness, to live lives that are easily distinguishable from those of the world around us.

How are you doing? Are you reflecting the holiness of God? Is your life so separate from and different than the world around you that it is like the difference between light and darkness?

As we saw in week 1, one of the tasks of the priests was to teach the people to distinguish between the unclean and the clean. In week 2 we learned that God's people, the Israelites, were not to be like everyone else. They were set apart unto God. This distinction was to be evident in every area of their lives, even down to the food they ate.

OBSERVE

The Israelites were commanded to make a clear distinction between the things that are *holy* and the things that are *common*. In Leviticus chapter 11 Moses taught his people the difference between the clean and unclean in regard to food, which would be one of the distinguishing marks between the Jewish nation and their pagan neighbors.

Leader: *Read Leviticus 11:41–47 aloud. Have the group do the following:*
  • *underline each occurrence of the phrase* **for I am the Lord.**
  • *draw a box around each occurrence of the phrase* **be holy, for I am holy.**

Leader: *Read through the passage again. This time have the group...*

LEVITICUS 11:41–47

41 "Now every swarming thing that swarms on the earth is detestable, not to be eaten.

42 "Whatever crawls on its belly, and whatever walks on all fours, whatever has many feet, in respect to every swarming thing that swarms on the earth, you shall not eat them, for they are detestable.

43 "Do not render yourselves detestable through any of the swarming things that

swarm; and you shall not make yourselves unclean with them so that you become unclean.

44 "For I am the LORD your God. Consecrate yourselves therefore, and be holy, for I am holy. And you shall not make yourselves unclean with any of the swarming things that swarm on the earth.

45 "For I am the LORD who brought you up from the land of Egypt to be your God; thus you shall be holy, for I am holy."

46 This is the law regarding the animal and the bird, and every living thing that moves in the waters

• *mark each occurrence of the word* **detestable** *with a cloud with a slash through it, like this:*

• *draw a cloud around the word* **distinction:**

INSIGHT

To *consecrate* something is to devote or set it apart to the worship and service of God. The Hebrew word for consecrate has the same root as the word *holy*.

DISCUSS

• Discuss what you learned about God from these verses.

• What was the Lord asking the people to do, and what did that mean exactly?

• According to verse 44, why was God telling them to do this?

• Discuss what right or authority God had to ask them to do this and what their obligation was to Him. What had He done for them? What did He expect in return?

• According to verse 47, what were they to make a distinction between?

• Was God primarily concerned about the people's physical health in these verses? Explain your answer.

and everything that swarms on the earth,

47 to make a distinction between the unclean and the clean, and between the edible creature and the creature which is not to be eaten.

LEVITICUS 20:22–26

22 You are therefore to keep all My statutes and all My ordinances and do them, so that the land to which I am bringing you to live will not spew you out.

23 Moreover, you shall not follow the customs of the nation which I will drive out before you, for they did all these things, and therefore I have abhorred them.

24 Hence I have said to you, "You are to possess their land, and I Myself will give it to you to possess it, a land flowing with milk and honey." I am the LORD your God, who has separated you from the peoples.

OBSERVE

Leader: *Read Leviticus 20:22–26 aloud. Have the group say and…*

- *draw a box around* **be holy to Me.**
- *underline the phrases* **I am the Lord your God** *and* **I the Lord am holy.**
- *draw a cloud around each occurrence of* **separated, distinction,** *and* **set you apart.**

DISCUSS

• Make a list of the instructions given to the nation of Israel in this passage.

• What did you learn from marking all the references to being separated and set apart?

• According to verse 26, what was the nation of Israel commanded to do, and why?

• From what you have seen in this passage, how do you become holy? Does your holiness depend simply on the food you eat or don't eat? Explain your answer, keeping in mind everything you have seen in this study.

• God is the great separator. According to verses 24 and 26, what has He separated Israel from, and why?

• What principles do we see in this passage that would apply to believers today? Think about it and discuss your answer.

25 You are therefore to make a distinction between the clean animal and the unclean, and between the unclean bird and the clean; and you shall not make yourselves detestable by animal or by bird or by anything that creeps on the ground, which I have separated for you as unclean.

26 Thus you are to be holy to Me, for I the LORD am holy; and I have set you apart from the peoples to be Mine.

2 CORINTHIANS 6:14–7:1

14 Do not be bound together with unbelievers; for what partnership have righteousness and lawlessness, or what fellowship has light with darkness?

15 Or what harmony has Christ with Belial, or what has a believer in common with an unbeliever?

16 Or what agreement has the temple of God with idols? For we are the temple of the living God; just as God said, "I will dwell in them and walk among them; and I will be their God, and they shall be My people.

17 "Therefore, come out from their midst and be separate," says

OBSERVE

Today we don't view animals as being unclean, but the New Testament does identify certain things as unclean. In this next passage Paul alluded to Leviticus 11.

Leader: *Read 2 Corinthians 6:14–7:1 aloud. Have the group say and...*

- *underline each **instruction**.*
- *draw a cloud around the phrase **be separate**.*

DISCUSS

- Discuss each instruction and how it relates to what we saw in Leviticus 11.

- Paul said that believers are not to be *bound together* with unbelievers. Why?

• What problems might this cause?

• If believers obeyed these instructions, what sort of problems might we avoid?

the Lord. "And do not touch what is unclean; and I will welcome you.

18 "And I will be a father to you, and you shall be sons and daughters to Me," says the Lord Almighty.

7:1 Therefore, having these promises, beloved, let us cleanse ourselves from all defilement of flesh and spirit, perfecting holiness in the fear of God.

1 PETER 1:14–16

14 As obedient children, do not be conformed to the former lusts which were yours in your ignorance,

15 but like the Holy One who called you, be holy yourselves also in all your behavior;

16 because it is written, "You shall be holy, for I am holy."

OBSERVE

As believers we are to be different from the world around us. Salvation should result in a lifestyle much different from our previous one.

Leader: Read 1 Peter 1:14–16 aloud. Have the group…

- *underline each __instruction.__*
- *draw a cloud around the word **holy.***

DISCUSS

- What are believers instructed to do here?

- The word *but* signals a contrast is taking place. What two things are being contrasted in these verses?

- As God's children we should reflect His character. What about you? Do people look at you and see Him in all your behavior?

• Does your lifestyle look the same as before you came to Christ? Or does it reflect the nature of the One who gave you new birth and called you to be His own?

OBSERVE

God often reminded the Israelites that He was the One who brought them out of Egypt, the one who set them free. Therefore they were to be holy. Just as the Passover was instituted as a way to remember what God had done for the Israelites, so the Lord's Supper, or Communion, was instituted for the church to remember what Christ has done for us and, therefore, to keep in mind our responsibility to be holy.

Leader: Read 1 Corinthians 11:23–26 aloud. Have the group say and…
- *draw a box around every reference to* **bread,** *including pronouns.*
- *circle every reference to* **the cup,** *including pronouns.*
- *draw a squiggly line like this under* ⁓⁓⁓⁓ *each occurrence of the phrase* **in remembrance of me.**

1 CORINTHIANS 11:23–26

23 For I received from the Lord that which I also delivered to you, that the Lord Jesus in the night in which He was betrayed took bread;

24 and when He had given thanks, He broke it and said, "This is My body, which is for you; do this in remembrance of Me."

25 In the same way He took the cup also after supper, saying, "This cup is the new covenant in My blood;

do this, as often as you drink it, in remembrance of Me."

26 For as often as you eat this bread and drink the cup, you proclaim the Lord's death until He comes.

DISCUSS

• Discuss what you learn from marking *bread* and *cup* in this passage.

• What are we to do each time we share the bread and the cup?

INSIGHT

The phrase *in remembrance of Me* reflects the Old Testament idea of *zikkaron*, or *memorial*. The Lord's Supper is a unique, holy occasion for the gathered church to remember each member's participation with Jesus in His death. The result should be that we live in a way that reflects Christ's sacrifice.

• How does remembering Christ's death affect your life? Is it simply a historical fact to you, or does it have some sort of impact on your choices?

• According to verse 26, what are you proclaiming when you participate in Communion, and for how long? Explain how this relates to all we have studied so far.

OBSERVE

The members of the Corinthian church were good at examining the lives of those around them. But like many Christians today, they weren't as good at examining their own lives.

Leader: Read 1 Corinthians 11:27–32 aloud. Have the group...
  • *draw a box around every occurrence of* **eat** *and* **eats.**
  • *circle every occurrence of* **drink** *and* **drinks.**
  • *mark the words* **judgment, judge,** *and* **judged** *with a* **J.**

DISCUSS

• If someone participates in the Lord's Supper in an unworthy manner, what is he guilty of? Explain your answer.

1 CORINTHIANS 11:27–32

27 Therefore whoever eats the bread or drinks the cup of the Lord in an unworthy manner, shall be guilty of the body and the blood of the Lord.

28 But a man must examine himself, and in so doing he is to eat of the bread and drink of the cup.

29 For he who eats and drinks, eats and drinks judgment to himself if he does not judge the body rightly.

30 For this reason many among you are

weak and sick, and a number sleep.

31 But if we judged ourselves rightly, we would not be judged.

32 But when we are judged, we are disciplined by the Lord so that we will not be condemned along with the world.

• According to verse 28, what is each person to do prior to participating in the Lord's Supper? Why?

• What are the consequences of not doing this?

• In light of all we have seen concerning holiness this week, what should observing the Lord's Supper encourage us to do?

WRAP IT UP

God is holy, and He delivered His people from Egypt so that they could be His holy people, His priestly nation revealing to a watching world that He is God. For this reason God continually told His people to live differently. Every aspect of their lives, even down to the foods they ate, was to be different from the people around them.

It is no different for us today. The people of God are called on to maintain the holiness He has already granted us through His grace. God still says, in essence, "Live differently, because I have made you different. Be what you are." Holiness is not something to be achieved by our own strenuous efforts. It is a state already created and given by God to His people.

> But you did not learn Christ in this way, if indeed you have heard
> Him and have been taught in Him, just as truth is in Jesus, that, in
> reference to your former manner of life, you lay aside the old self,
> which is being corrupted in accordance with the lusts of deceit,
> and that you be renewed in the spirit of your mind, and put on
> the new self, which in the likeness of God has been created in
> righteousness and holiness of the truth. (Ephesians 4:20–24)

As you continue to immerse yourself in the Word of God, as you are doing in this study, you are renewed in the spirit of your mind. The end result is that you are putting on the new self, created in the likeness of God.

However, it seems some Christians have forgotten all Christ has done for them and failed to be distinctively different from the world around them. They have not engaged in the Word so as to have the spirit of their mind renewed. The result is the church has been influenced by the world and its views rather than impacting the world with the truth of God. Too many times the church looks like the culture surrounding it. It seems the church has become a thermometer, measuring the temperature of the world, when we should be a thermostat, setting the temperature to holiness.

Remember: You belong to God. Be holy, because He is holy.

The Old Testament teaches that God, the Law, the temple, and the nation of Israel are all holy. But does any of that apply to us now? What about Christians? Believers are called *saints*, but what does that mean?

OBSERVE

In his letter to various young churches, Peter described the incredible blessings of salvation and then turned his attention to how we are to live in light of those blessings.

Leader: Read 1 Peter 1:13–16 aloud. Have the group say and…
- *circle each occurrence of the words **you, your,** and **yourselves.***
- *draw a cloud around each occurrence of the word **holy:***

Leader: Read the passage again and have the group underline each **instruction.**

DISCUSS

- As obedient children, what were these believers instructed to do?

1 PETER 1:13–16

13 Therefore, prepare your minds for action, keep sober in spirit, fix your hope completely on the grace to be brought to you at the revelation of Jesus Christ.

14 As obedient children, do not be conformed to the former lusts which were yours in your ignorance,

15 but like the Holy One who called you, be holy yourselves also in all your behavior;

16 because it is written, "You shall be holy, for I am holy."

• How should their obedience to these instructions affect their lifestyle, and why? Explain your answer.

• As God's children, what key characteristics are we to demonstrate? Who are we to be like?

---

1 PETER 2:9–10

9 But you are a chosen race, a royal priesthood, a holy nation, a people for God's own possession, so that you may proclaim the excellencies of Him who has called you out of darkness into His marvelous light;

10 for you once were not a people, but now

OBSERVE

Leader: Read 1 Peter 2:9–10 aloud and have the group…

• *circle each occurrence of the word **you**.*
• *draw a cloud around the word **holy**.*

DISCUSS

• What did you learn from marking *you*?

• What is God's purpose for choosing us?

• Peter's wording here—"you are…so that you may"—makes it clear that with the privilege of being God's chosen possession comes responsibility. What is this responsibility, and how does it apply to your life today?

OBSERVE

How can believers proclaim God's excellencies to others?

Leader: Read 1 Peter 2:11–12 and Matthew 5:16. Have the group say and…

- *circle each occurrence of the words **you** and **your.***
- *underline each **instruction.***

INSIGHT

By using the phrase *aliens and strangers,* Peter is saying this world is not our home. Our real home is heaven.

The word *Gentiles* in 1 Peter 2:12 is a synonym for *non-Christians.*

1 PETER 2:11–12

you are the people of God; you had not received mercy, but now you have received mercy.

11 Beloved, I urge you as aliens and strangers to abstain from fleshly lusts which wage war against the soul.

12 Keep your behavior excellent among the Gentiles, so that in the thing in which they slander you as evildoers, they may because of your good deeds, as they observe them, glorify God in the day of visitation.

Matthew 5:16

Let your light shine before men in such a way that they may see your good works, and glorify your Father who is in heaven.

DISCUSS

• What instructions did Peter give the believers?

• Practically speaking, what does it mean to lives as aliens and strangers in today's culture?

• According to 1 Peter 2:12 and Matthew 5:16, what will your good deeds as a believer accomplish? Who do they prove you belong to?

• Have you ever heard someone say, "I am not going to that church, because it's full of hypocrites"? What does that tell you about the lifestyle of some of the people who attend that church and what effect does it have on the unsaved?

• What about your lifestyle? Would you be labeled as a hypocrite? Why or why not?

OBSERVE

Another indication of holiness in the life of a believer is how that person responds to authority.

Leader: Read 1 Peter 2:13–17 aloud. Have the group say and...
- *circle each occurrence of the words* **yourselves, you,** *and* **your.**
- *underline each* **instruction.**

DISCUSS

- What did Peter call for the believers to do in verses 13–15?

- Generally speaking, what is the purpose of authority?

- What if the individual who holds that office is ungodly or if you don't respect the man or woman holding that office? Do you still have to submit? Explain your answer.

1 PETER 2:13–17

13 Submit yourselves for the Lord's sake to every human institution, whether to a king as the one in authority,

14 or to governors as sent by him for the punishment of evildoers and the praise of those who do right.

15 For such is the will of God that by doing right you may silence the ignorance of foolish men.

16 Act as free men, and do not use your freedom as a covering for evil, but use it as bondslaves of God.

17 Honor all people, love the brotherhood, fear God, honor the king.

• What will be the result of a believer's practice of holiness, according to verse 15?

• What is to be our motivation for obedience? Avoiding punishment? Explain your answer from this passage.

• What was Peter's concern in verse 16?

• Discuss the four points Peter makes in verse 17 and how each relates to a believer's behavior as a citizen.

ROMANS 13:1–7

¹ Every person is to be in subjection to the governing authorities. For there is no authority except from God, and those which exist are established by God.

OBSERVE

Leader: *Read Romans 13:1–7 aloud and have the group...*

- *underline each reference to **authority**, including synonyms such as **rulers** and pronouns such as **those**.*
- *circle every reference to **believers**, including the phrase **every person** and the pronoun **you**.*

To be *in subjection* is to place one-self under the authority of another.

DISCUSS

• Who is to submit to authorities?

• Where does all authority (good and bad) come from?

• According to verse 2, what is the one who resists authority doing and what will be the consequence?

• Look at every place you marked *authority* in verses 3–7 and discuss what you learned.

2 Therefore whoever resists authority has opposed the ordinance of God; and they who have opposed will receive condemnation upon themselves.

3 For rulers are not a cause of fear for good behavior, but for evil. Do you want to have no fear of authority? Do what is good and you will have praise from the same;

4 for it is a minister of God to you for good. But if you do what is evil, be afraid; for it does not bear the sword for nothing; for it is a minister of God, an avenger who brings wrath on the one who practices evil.

5 Therefore it is necessary to be in subjection, not only because of wrath, but also for conscience' sake.

6 For because of this you also pay taxes, for rulers are servants of God, devoting themselves to this very thing.

7 Render to all what is due them: tax to whom tax is due; custom to whom custom; fear to whom fear; honor to whom honor.

• Why is it necessary to submit to all authority?

• According to verses 6 and 7, what is a believer's responsibility to authorities besides obedience?

• In addition to support by paying taxes, what else is to be given?

• Explain how submitting to authorities and honoring them relates to our study on holiness.

OBSERVE

In Romans 12:10, Paul gets to the heart of how holiness is demonstrated in our behavior toward others.

Leader: Read Romans 12:10 aloud.
- *Have the group say aloud and circle each occurrence of the phrase **one another**.*

DISCUSS

- What did you see about how believers are to behave toward one another?

- Discuss some practical examples of what this would look like.

ROMANS 12:10

Be devoted to one another in brotherly love; give preference to one another in honor.

WRAP IT UP

The term *chosen people*, which used to apply only to Israel, is now used for both Jewish and Gentile believers. The responsibility to reflect God's holiness, once entrusted solely to the nation of Israel, has now been given to the church as well. God said to the descendants of Jacob, the people of Israel: "You shall be to Me a kingdom of priests and a holy nation" (Exodus 19:6). Now believers are called "a chosen race, a royal priesthood, a holy nation, a people for God's own possession" (1 Peter 2:9). Peter also called Christians "a holy priesthood" (2:5).

God's purpose in choosing believers for Himself is so that they may declare His praises before others. Believers should live so that their heavenly Father's qualities are evident in their lives. They are to serve as witnesses of the glory and grace of God, who called them "out of darkness into His marvelous light" (1 Peter 2:9).

So then, in practicing holiness we are reflecting God's character to the world around us. All of our behavior must be pleasing to God, including our submission to authority. Following God does not give us the right to resist or defy the secular authority He has placed over us. God has established all authority, and by respecting the office and honoring authority we show the world that we honor God. In other words, being under authority is reflecting holiness. However, we are always to be careful never to allow the law of the land to overrule the law of the Lord.

How are you doing? Are you paying your taxes? Obeying the speed limits? Obeying the law? Honoring those officials placed in authority over you, such as the president? Your supervisor at work?

"Let your light shine before men in such a way that they may see your good works, and glorify your Father who is in heaven" (Matthew 5:16).

Be holy, because I am holy. As those who belong to God, we are called to the practice of holiness. The call is based on the character of God Himself. This week we'll consider further what it looks like to practice holiness in our dealings with others.

OBSERVE

Leader: *Read aloud the verses on this page. Have the group say aloud and…*

- *underline each occurrence of the word* **temple.**
- *draw a cloud around the word* **holy:**

DISCUSS

- What did you learn from marking *temple*?

- What word does 1 Corinthians 3:17 use to describe the temple of God? How does that designation apply to you?

1 CORINTHIANS 3:16–17

16 Do you not know that you are a temple of God and that the Spirit of God dwells in you?

17 If any man destroys the temple of God, God will destroy him, for the temple of God is holy, and that is what you are.

1 CORINTHIANS 6:19

Or do you not know that your body is a temple of the Holy Spirit who is in you, whom you have from God, and that you are not your own?

ROMANS 1:7

To all who are beloved of God in Rome, called as saints: Grace to you and peace from God our Father and the Lord Jesus Christ.

1 CORINTHIANS 1:2

To the church of God which is at Corinth, to those who have been sanctified in Christ Jesus, saints by calling, with all who in every place call on the name of our Lord Jesus Christ, their Lord and ours.

OBSERVE

In these next two verses notice how Paul describes the two different churches to whom he is writing.

Leader: Read Romans 1:7 and 1 Corinthians 1:2 aloud. Have the group…
- *underline the phrases **to all who are beloved of God** and **to the church of God.***
- *draw a cloud around each occurrence of the word **saints.***

INSIGHT

Saint means "one who is holy or set apart." The term implies separation and devotion to the service of God.

DISCUSS

- Specifically, who was Paul addressing in each of these verses?

- What are they called?

• Do you think of yourself as a saint? Why or why not?

• If you are a saint, how should that knowledge impact your daily life?

OBSERVE

The apostle John wrote a clear description of God's character and what that means for those who worship Him.

Leader: *Read 1 John 1:5–7 aloud.*
  • *Have the group mark every reference to **God,** including pronouns, with a triangle:* △

INSIGHT

In the Bible light is often a symbol of God and His holiness, while darkness represents evil and sin.

1 JOHN 1:5–7

5 This is the message we have heard from Him and announce to you, that God is Light, and in Him there is no darkness at all.

6 If we say that we have fellowship with Him and yet walk in the darkness, we lie and do not practice the truth;

7 but if we walk in the Light as He Himself is in the Light, we have

fellowship with one another, and the blood of Jesus His Son cleanses us from all sin.

DISCUSS

• What did you learn about God in verse 5, and what does that mean?

• What did you learn about the relationship between God and believers? Explain how this relates to what we have seen in our study so far.

JOHN 8:12

Then Jesus again spoke to them, saying, "I am the Light of the world; he who follows Me will not walk in the darkness, but will have the Light of life."

OBSERVE

John 8 records part of Jesus' public teaching in the temple area during the Feast of Tabernacles. At this time the large lamps were burning in remembrance of God's leading the Israelites out of the wilderness by a pillar of fire. What an object lesson!

Leader: Read John 8:12 aloud and have the group...

* *mark each reference to **Jesus,** including pronouns, with a cross:* †
* *draw a semicircle over every occurrence of the word **Light,** like this:* ⌒

DISCUSS

• What did you learn about Jesus in this verse?

• From all you have seen in Scripture, what distinguishes a believer's lifestyle from that of the world around him?

OBSERVE

Let's next look at a passage in which Paul addressed the believers in Ephesus who were learning how to live a holy lifestyle.

Leader: *Read Ephesians 5:8–13 aloud. Have the group say and…*
   • *draw a semicircle over every occurrence of the word* **Light.**
   • *underline each* **_instruction._**

EPHESIANS 5:8–13

8 For you were formerly darkness, but now you are Light in the Lord; walk as children of Light

9 (for the fruit of the Light consists in all goodness and righteousness and truth),

10 trying to learn what is pleasing to the Lord.

11 Do not participate in the unfruitful deeds of darkness, but instead even expose them;

12 for it is disgraceful even to speak of the things which are done by them in secret.

13 But all things become visible when they are exposed by the light, for everything that becomes visible is light.

DISCUSS

• What contrast did Paul make in verse 8?

• What instruction did he give in connection with that contrast?

• Discuss each aspect of this new lifestyle as listed in verses 9–11 and how it should look in the life of a believer.

• According to verse 11, what were these new believers to do?

• What is the result of light shining in a person's heart?

OBSERVE

In Leviticus God told the Israelites to "be holy, for I am holy" (11:45). Now we as believers are told to "walk as children of Light" (Ephesians 5:8). It is really the same thing.

We already read Ephesians 5:9, which describes the fruit of the Light. In Galatians 5, Paul contrasted walking in the flesh with walking in the Spirit. He also described the fruit of those who walk in the Spirit.

Leader: Read Galatians 5:22–25 aloud and have the group…

- *underline the word **fruit.***
- *number each **fruit of the Spirit.** The first is marked for you.*

DISCUSS

- Who produces this fruit—the believer or the Spirit?

- Discuss how this fruit is produced.

GALATIANS 5:22–25

22 But the fruit of the Spirit is love, joy, peace, patience, kindness, goodness, faithfulness,

23 gentleness, self-control; against such things there is no law.

24 Now those who belong to Christ Jesus have crucified the flesh with its passions and desires.

25 If we live by the Spirit, let us also walk by the Spirit.

INSIGHT

Love—self-sacrificing for the benefit of the one loved.

Joy—a deep inner rejoicing that doesn't depend on circumstances.

Peace—an inner quietness even in the face of difficult circumstances.

Patience—Long-suffering. Self-restraint when provoked.

Kindness—a disposition that is mellow, not harsh and cutting.

Goodness—doing good to others even when it is not deserved.

Faithfulness—trustworthy or reliable

Gentleness—right use of power and authority. Considerate of others even when discipline is needed.

Self-control—controlling one's actions, feelings, impulses, etc.

- What should this fruit look like in the life of a believer, and how should it be lived out?

OBSERVE

In Jesus' teaching in the Sermon on the Mount, a recurring theme is the distinctiveness of the believer.

Leader: Read Matthew 5:43–48 aloud.
- *Have the group circle each occurrence of* **you** *and* **your**.

Leader: Read the passage again.
- *This time have the group underline each* **instruction** *Jesus gave in these verses.*

DISCUSS

- As we've noted before, the word *but* often points to a contrast being made. Specifically, what two teachings are being contrasted in this passage?

- From what you read in verses 44 and 45, what specifically does Jesus want His followers to do, and why?

MATTHEW 5:43–48

43 You have heard that it was said, "You shall love your neighbor and hate your enemy."

44 But I say to you, love your enemies and pray for those who persecute you,

45 so that you may be sons of your Father who is in heaven; for He causes His sun to rise on the evil and the good, and sends rain on the righteous and the unrighteous.

46 For if you love those who love you, what reward do you have? Do not even the tax collectors do the same?

47 If you greet only your brothers, what more are you doing than others? Do not even the Gentiles do the same?

48 Therefore you are to be perfect, as your heavenly Father is perfect.

• According to verse 48, as believers what should our goal be?

• Taking into consideration all you have studied so far, what should our standard of living be? Explain your answer.

• Since we are learning the practice of holiness, how are we to respond to those we are naturally inclined to hate? Those who persecute us?

• Examine yourself. Are you growing in holiness, understanding more about God and His ways? Is the fruit of the Spirit evident in your life?

WRAP IT UP

The practice of holiness leaves little room for personal comfort or even personal concern. Our practice of holiness is to be God-centered and people-focused. We are not to be distracted by selfish concerns. *We are to be holy as He is holy.*

Each aspect of the fruit of the Spirit is seen in relation to others. In fact the only way to prove that holiness even exists in our lives is to live it out in relationship with others. The practice of holiness would be easy if it were not for the people we all have to interact with!

That prompts us to leave you with a challenge: close today by praying through the fruit of the Spirit, asking God to produce this fruit in your own life. But please understand, the moment you do this He will begin a process in your life of causing you to die to your own self-centeredness and training you to practice holiness by putting Him first, all others second, and yourself a distant third.

Are you up for the challenge?

In week 4 we examined 1 Peter 2:13–17 and saw that the practice of holiness involves being under the governmental authorities. In week 5 we looked at what it means to walk as children of Light in our daily interactions.

This week, as we walk through more of 1 Peter, we will continue to look at how the practice of holiness should affect our relationships with the people in our lives, including those in authority over us, even in the face of injustice and suffering.

OBSERVE

Servants and slaves made up a large percentage of the early church. Today we may view passages addressed to them through the lens of our dealings with an employer or other authority figures.

Leader: Read 1 Peter 2:18–20 aloud. Have the group say aloud and...

- *put an **S** over each reference to **servants,** including pronouns.*
- *mark every reference to **God** with a triangle:* △

1 PETER 2:18–20

18 Servants, be submissive to your masters with all respect, not only to those who are good and gentle, but also to those who are unreasonable.

19 For this finds favor, if for the sake of conscience toward God a person bears up under sorrows when suffering unjustly.

20 For what credit is there if, when you sin and are harshly treated, you endure it with patience? But if when you do what is right and suffer for it you patiently endure it, this finds favor with God.

DISCUSS

• What are servants called to do in verse 18? How?

• Are they to submit only to a good master?

• Discuss what you learned about being submissive to the unreasonable master.

• Why should believers patiently endure injustice? What does it result in?

• Typically what is our natural reaction to injustice?

• How does that compare with what we have seen?

OBSERVE

Leader: Read Romans 12:19–21 aloud. Have the group…

- *draw a box around each occurrence of the word **but:*** ☐
- *mark every reference to **God**, including synonyms and pronouns, with a triangle.*

DISCUSS

- According to verse 19, what was Paul's advice to believers who are victims of injustice?

- Discuss how they are to respond instead and what that means in practical terms.

- In light of God's promise to execute justice, what should the believer do?

ROMANS 12:19–21

19 Never take your own revenge, beloved, but leave room for the wrath of God, for it is written, "Vengeance is Mine, I will repay," says the Lord.

20 "But if your enemy is hungry, feed him, and if he is thirsty, give him a drink; for in so doing you will heap burning coals on his head."

21 Do not be overcome by evil, but overcome evil with good.

• What is Paul's instruction in verse 21, and how does that relate to what you saw in verse 20 as well as 1 Peter 2:18–20?

1 PETER 2:21–25

21 For you have been called for this purpose, since Christ also suffered for you, leaving you an example for you to follow in His steps,

22 who committed no sin, nor was any deceit found in His mouth;

23 and while being reviled, He did not revile in return; while suffering, He uttered no threats, but kept entrusting Himself to Him who judges righteously;

OBSERVE

Let's return to 1 Peter 2 and Peter's teaching about how to respond when we suffer for doing good. Following his advice to the slaves, he pointed to the powerful example of Christ's endurance under unjust suffering.

Leader: Read 1 Peter 2:21–25 aloud. Have the group…
  • *circle the pronouns **you, our, we,** and **your,** which refer here to **believers.***
  • *mark each reference to **Christ,** including synonyms and pronouns, with a cross:* †

DISCUSS

• In the midst of His suffering, what did Christ provide for us?

• How did Peter describe Christ in verse 22?

• With Jesus' example in mind, how are we to respond in the face of suffering?

• Discuss what you learned about Christ through His example and how every aspect relates to us as believers.

• According to verses 24 and 25, what did His death make possible?

24 and He Himself bore our sins in His body on the cross, so that we might die to sin and live to righteousness; for by His wounds you were healed.

25 For you were continually straying like sheep, but now you have returned to the Shepherd and Guardian of your souls.

• Peter was not teaching that we are saved by following Christ's example; he was saying that, because we are saved, we are to follow His example. How do you respond when you suffer injustice? How will you respond in the future? Think about it.

1 PETER 3:1–6

1 In the same way, you wives, be submissive to your own husbands so that even if any of them are disobedient to the word, they may be won without a word by the behavior of their wives,

2 as they observe your chaste and respectful behavior.

3 Your adornment must not be merely external—braiding the

OBSERVE

Peter addressed how believers should practice holiness in some of their relationships with the world. Now he begins to deal with the practice of holiness in the family. The phrase *in the same way* here refers back to what we saw in week 4 in 1 Peter 2:13–17: "Submit yourselves for the Lord's sake to every human institution."

Leader: Read the following passages aloud, ending with Colossians 3:18, and have the group…

• *circle every reference to **wives**, including pronouns.*
• *draw a squiggly line like this under each occurrence of the word **behavior**.*

DISCUSS

• What instruction is given to wives in these passages?

• According to 1 Peter 3:1–2, what will the result be?

• Does this apply to women who are married to unbelievers? Explain your answer.

• From what you have seen, what is the best way for a woman to win her unbelieving husband to the Lord?

• Describe the character qualities of a godly (holy) wife.

hair, and wearing gold jewelry, or putting on dresses;

4 but let it be the hidden person of the heart, with the imperishable quality of a gentle and quiet spirit, which is precious in the sight of God.

5 For in this way in former times the holy women also, who hoped in God, used to adorn themselves, being submissive to their own husbands;

6 just as Sarah obeyed Abraham, calling him lord, and you have become her children if you do what is right without being frightened by any fear.

EPHESIANS 5:22

Wives, be subject to your own husbands, as to the Lord.

COLOSSIANS 3:18

Wives, be subject to your husbands, as is fitting in the Lord.

1 PETER 3:7

You husbands in the same way, live with your wives in an understanding way, as with someone weaker, since she is a woman; and show her honor as a fellow heir of the grace of life, so that your prayers will not be hindered.

• From what you saw in the verses from Ephesians and Colossians, how is this submission to be carried out? Explain your answer.

• What kind of an impact would it have on the culture if women would actually model this kind of behavior?

OBSERVE

Leader: Read the following passages aloud.
  • *Have the group draw a box around every reference to **husbands**, including pronouns.*

DISCUSS

• What two things are husbands instructed to do in their relationship with their wives, according to 1 Peter 3:7?

INSIGHT

The phrase *live with your wives in an understanding way* here points to the fact that a husband should understand and be considerate of his wife's emotional, physical, and spiritual needs.

Weaker here refers to a woman's physical condition, not her emotions or intellect. And it certainly does not imply inferiority.

The Greek word translated here as *love* is *agape. Agape* love is sacrificial and has in mind the highest good of the one being loved. It is not an emotional type of love; rather it is a love of action.

EPHESIANS 5:25

Husbands, love your wives, just as Christ also loved the church and gave Himself up for her.

COLOSSIANS 3:19

Husbands, love your wives and do not be embittered against them.

• Discuss what it would look like for a believer to obey the instructions to *live with your wives in an understanding way* and *show her honor.*

• What can the husband expect if he does not show his wife understanding and honor?

• From what you saw in Ephesians and Colossians, what else is the husband instructed to do?

• Who is the husband's example and what behavior is he to imitate? Explain your answer.

OBSERVE

How are believers to behave in the midst of a hostile culture? We are to be holy. Peter explains how we can live in ways that are countercultural. In doing so we will be distinct from the world around us, and that distinction will reflect the Holy One who has called us.

Leader: Read 1 Peter 3:8–9 aloud.
  *• Have the group circle each occurrence of the word **you,** which refers to **believers.***

DISCUSS

• Discuss the characteristics of holy living seen in this passage and how they should affect a believer's behavior in the midst of a hostile world.

• According to verse 9, how would God's holiness be seen in a believer's life?

1 PETER 3:8–9

8 To sum up, all of you be harmonious, sympathetic, brotherly, kindhearted, and humble in spirit;

9 not returning evil for evil or insult for insult, but giving a blessing instead; for you were called for the very purpose that you might inherit a blessing.

WRAP IT UP

God did not spare Christ but sacrificed Him to pay for our sins. The only appropriate response is to sacrifice ourselves for Him. He gave all for us, we give all for Him.

The practice of holiness will only become a reality in your life when you care more about God than you do about yourself. As we take daily steps to glorify God, His holiness is seen in our separation from the concerns and distractions of this world, in our separation to our holy God.

The practice of holiness is not for the weak or the fainthearted. It is the day-to-day life of those who are filled with the presence of the Holy One of Israel and who, by His power, are losing concern for themselves. As we lose our self-centeredness and grow in our love of God we will begin to practice holiness. Our love for Him is shown not only in our commitment to right living but also in our love for people.

How are you doing in this? Are you living every moment of every day to glorify the God of glory? Is He the most important thing in your life? If He is, if you are seeking to bring glory to His name and to live like you belong to Him, then your life will be marked by love for others.

Go now and practice holiness.

40
MINUTE
BIBLE
STUDIES

No-Homework
That Help You

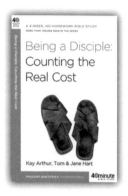

A 6-WEEK, NO-HOMEWORK BIBLE STUDY
MORE THAN 700,000 SOLD IN THE SERIES

Being a Disciple:
Counting the
Real Cost

Kay Arthur, Tom & Jane Hart

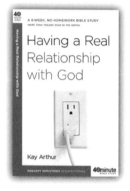

A 6-WEEK, NO-HOMEWORK BIBLE STUDY
MORE THAN 700,000 SOLD IN THE SERIES

Having a Real
Relationship
with God

Kay Arthur

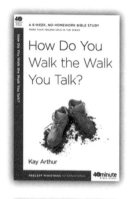

A 6-WEEK, NO-HOMEWORK BIBLE STUDY
MORE THAN 700,000 SOLD IN THE SERIES

How Do You
Walk the Walk
You Talk?

Kay Arthur

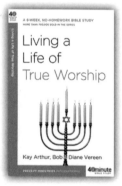

A 6-WEEK, NO-HOMEWORK BIBLE STUDY
MORE THAN 700,000 SOLD IN THE SERIES

Living a
Life of
True Worship

Kay Arthur, Bob & Diane Vereen

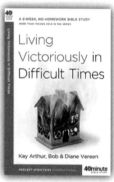

A 6-WEEK, NO-HOMEWORK BIBLE STUDY
MORE THAN 700,000 SOLD IN THE SERIES

Living
Victoriously in
Difficult Times

Kay Arthur, Bob & Diane Vereen

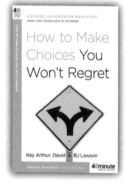

A 6-WEEK, NO-HOMEWORK BIBLE STUDY
MORE THAN 700,000 SOLD IN THE SERIES

How to Make
Choices You
Won't Regret

Kay Arthur, David & BJ Lawson

A 6-WEEK, NO-HOMEWORK BIBLE STUDY
MORE THAN 700,000 SOLD IN THE SERIES

Money and
Possessions:
The Quest for
Contentment

Kay Arthur & David Arthur

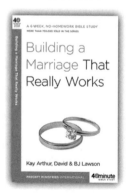

A 6-WEEK, NO-HOMEWORK BIBLE STUDY
MORE THAN 700,000 SOLD IN THE SERIES

Building a
Marriage That
Really Works

Kay Arthur, David & BJ Lawson

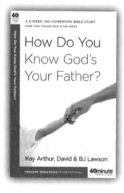

A 6-WEEK, NO-HOMEWORK BIBLE STUDY
MORE THAN 700,000 SOLD IN THE SERIES

How Do You
Know God's
Your Father?

Kay Arthur, David & BJ Lawson

Bible Studies
Discover Truth For Yourself

Discovering What the Future Holds

Kay Arthur & Georg Huber

Forgiveness: Breaking the Power of the Past

Kay Arthur, David & BJ Lawson

Living Like You Belong to God

Kay Arthur, David & BJ Lawson

The Essentials of Effective Prayer

Kay Arthur, David & BJ Lawson

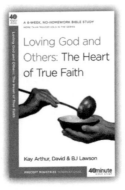

Loving God and Others: The Heart of True Faith

Kay Arthur, David & BJ Lawson

Understanding Spiritual Gifts

Kay Arthur, David and BJ Lawson

Also Available:

A Man's Strategy for Conquering Temptation
Rising to the Call of Leadership
Key Principles of Biblical Fasting
What Does the Bible Say About Sex?
Turning Your Heart Toward God
Fatal Distractions: Conquering Destructive Temptations
Spiritual Warfare: Overcoming the Enemy
The Power of Knowing God
Breaking Free from Fear

Another powerful study series from beloved Bible teacher

[A Devotional Study on Living by Faith]

LORD,
Where Are You
When Bad Things
Happen?

KAY ARTHUR

[A Devotional Study on Growing in Character from the Beatitudes]

LORD,
Only You
Can
Change Me

KAY ARTHUR

[A Devotional Study on Spiritual Victory]

LORD,
Is It Warfare?
Teach Me
to Stand

KAY ARTHUR

[A Devotional Study on the Names of God]

LORD,
I Want
to Know
You

KAY ARTHUR

[A Devotional Study on God's Power for Daily Living]

LORD,
I Need
Grace to
Make It Today

KAY ARTHUR

KAY ARTHUR

The Lord series provides insightful, warm-hearted Bible studies designed to meet you where you are—and help you discover God's answers to your deepest needs.

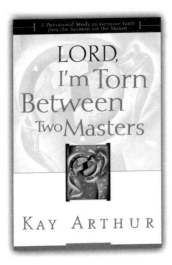

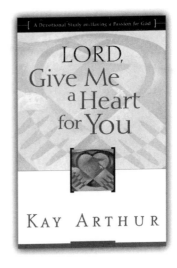

ALSO AVAILABLE:
One-year devotionals to draw you closer to the heart of God.

ABOUT KAY ARTHUR AND PRECEPT MINISTRIES INTERNATIONAL

KAY ARTHUR is known around the world as an international Bible teacher, author, conference speaker, and host of the national radio and television programs *Precepts for Life*, which reaches a worldwide viewing audience of over 94 million. A four-time Gold Medallion Award–winning author, Kay has authored more than 100 books and Bible studies.

Kay and her husband, Jack, founded Precept Ministries International in 1970 in Chattanooga, Tennessee, with a vision to establish people in God's Word. Today, the ministry has a worldwide outreach. In addition to inductive study training workshops and thousands of small-group studies across America, PMI reaches nearly 150 countries with inductive Bible studies translated into nearly 70 languages, teaching people to discover Truth for themselves.

Contact Precept Ministries International for more information about inductive Bible studies in your area.

Precept Ministries International
P.O. Box 182218
Chattanooga, TN 37422-7218
800-763-8280
www.precept.org

ABOUT DAVID AND BJ LAWSON

DAVID AND BJ LAWSON have been involved with Precept Ministries International since 1980. After nine years in the pastorate, they joined PMI full-time as directors of the student ministries and staff teachers and trainers. A featured speaker at PMI conferences and in Precept Upon Precept videos, David writes for the Precept Upon Precept series, the New Inductive Study Series, and the 40-Minute Bible Studies series. BJ has written numerous 40-Minute Bible Studies and serves as the chief editor and developer of the series. In addition she is a featured speaker at PMI women's conferences.